A MESSAGE FROM UKRAINE

A MESSAGE FROM UKRAINE

SPEECHES, 2019—2022

Volodymyr Zelensky

HUTCHINSON
HEINEMANN

1 3 5 7 9 10 8 6 4 2

Hutchinson Heinemann
20 Vauxhall Bridge Road
London SW1V 2SA

Hutchinson Heinemann is part of the Penguin Random House
group of companies whose addresses can be found at
global.penguinrandomhouse.com.

First published by Hutchinson Heinemann in 2022

www.penguin.co.uk

A CIP catalogue record for this book is available from the British Library.

ISBN 9781529153545

Typeset in 12/15pt Fournier MT Std by Jouve (UK), Milton Keynes.
Printed and bound in Great Britain by Clays Ltd, Elcograf S.p.A.

The authorised representative in the EEA is Penguin Random House Ireland,
Morrison Chambers, 32 Nassau Street, Dublin D02 YH68

www.greenpenguin.co.uk

Contents

Preface: We Are Here

Volodymyr Zelensky's most important speech was also his shortest. It lasted about thirty-two seconds and was delivered thirty-eight hours after Russia began an unprovoked all-out war against his country. Dressed in khaki, Zelensky filmed himself outside a government building on his phone. In the background stood various members of his senior team. 'Good evening, everyone,' he said. 'We are all here. Our soldiers are here. Civil society is here. We defend our independence. And this is how it will always be from now on.'

By the time the video appeared on social media on the evening of 25 February, Ukraine had been under relentless fire for more than a day, Russian paratroopers were storming a military airport in Kyiv, commandos were hunting for Zelensky and people were fleeing their homes. There were rumours – spread by Russian officials – that Zelensky had left the country and that his government had collapsed. This half-minute video proved otherwise.

In the hours, days and months that followed, Zelensky would address his country, the Russian people and the world over a hundred times. In the first two hundred days of the war, he gave eighty-one speeches to foreign audiences, and even more addressed to his own people. His speeches would draw comparisons with Churchill and his khaki T-shirt would become a global fashion icon. The Ukrainian flag would fly over government buildings and private homes across the Western world; the Brandenburg Gate and the Eiffel Tower would be lit in its yellow and blue.

But it was this short video that would have the greatest impact on the course of the war. It was proof that Putin's plan for a lightning-quick victory was failing; in fact, it had already failed. Zelensky did not run, the Ukrainian capital did not fall into Putin's hands, and people in the Russian-speaking east of the country did not welcome his troops with flowers. Zelensky was '*tut*': 'here', in his place, reporting for duty. And so was his country.

The President seemed like an unlikely war leader. He did not choose the part and did not prepare for it: in the weeks leading up to the invasion he even downplayed its likelihood. But when American officials offered him an airlift within hours of Putin's invasion, his reply was concise: 'I need ammo, not a ride.' His words became an instant meme, along with those of the Ukrainian defenders on the tiny Zmiinyi Island in the Black Sea when a Russian navy ship ordered them to surrender: 'Russian warship, go fuck yourself.'

Zelensky's simple rhetoric highlighted a stark contrast between the warring regimes. The short, warm word '*tut*' – repeated nine times in that first video's half-minute – felt like the kind of reassurance a parent might use to comfort a scared child whose house was being invaded. Zelensky's use of technology was also significant. Where Putin was a deluded dictator who broadcast at his subjects from behind the high walls of the Kremlin, Zelensky stood with his people. Posting a selfie video online showed Zelensky to be an everyman, an integral part of the social network that was Ukraine.

By February 2022, Zelensky had been President for just under three years. Voters had first known him as Vasyl Holoborodko, a plain-speaking history teacher who is miraculously catapulted into the job of President and takes on Ukraine's entire political system – the part Zelensky played in a television satire called *Servant of the People*. After launching his presidential campaign in December 2018, Zelensky's background as an actor and producer would prove crucial to his success. He knew how to mirror his audience, and voters recognised themselves in his likeness. He did not just speak at Ukrainians, he read their lips and articulated their feelings.

Suddenly, that ability was more important than ever. Ukraine had long been a people, a place, and, after the 1991 collapse of the Soviet Union, a state. Now, it was also becoming a civic nation: one defined not by language or ethnicity, nor by its ancient history or faith, but by its values, its way of life, and its people's readiness to die for it. Zelensky had once lent his voice to Paddington Bear in the Ukrainian dubs of *Paddington* and *Paddington 2*. Now, he was lending his voice to the Ukrainian people.

The birthplace of this nation was Maidan Nezalezhnosti – Independence Square – in Kyiv, the site of several revolutionary uprisings in which Ukrainians had come together to decide their own future. In 2014 they went there to say they belonged in Europe and to overthrow Viktor Yanukovych, a Moscow-backed thug who had tried to deny them this right. The revolution ended in violence. Yanukovych fled, and Russia annexed the Ukrainian territory of Crimea and started a war in the east of the country.

Zelensky was not on Maidan in 2014 and did not participate in what became known as the 'Revolution of Dignity', although he did call on Yanukovych to step down. It was not that he disagreed with the protestors' demands; rather that he was driven by neither nationalism nor ideology, and, stylistically, revolutions were not his 'genre'. As a successful television producer he had a strong sense of his audience – slightly cynical, self-reliant, conformist but also deeply grounded. During the revolution, much of this audience stayed at home watching his sitcoms.

But while Zelensky was not a participant in the Maidan uprising, his political career was a reaction to its broken promises. Like much of the country, he cringed when politicians used lofty language while scheming for their own financial advantage, and was appalled when the old elites regrouped, wrapped themselves in new banners and went back to their old ways. But while the establishment carried on as before, the country was changing; its civil society was growing and it was no longer prepared to put up with business as usual. In 2019, Ukrainians rebuked the corrupt post-Soviet elite by voting for Holoborodko – aka Zelensky – as President.

The idea of an outsider bursting into an oligarchic

system where money decided everything – and where owning a television station, a bank and a small private army was usually a prerequisite for political power – seemed almost as improbable a story as Holoborodko's. But Ukrainians have a taste for the improbable. A pro-Ukrainian Russian speaker from a Jewish family in Eastern Ukraine, Zelensky received the votes of three quarters of the electorate across the entire country. Never before had the electoral map of Ukraine looked so cohesive.

Some liberals in Ukraine and Ukraine-watchers in the West were sceptical about Zelensky's victory. They expressed concern about his lack of either a comprehensive programme or a professional team. But what Zelensky lacked in political experience, he made up for in his sense of humour, his chutzpah and his communication skills – a set of assets that were essential in post-Soviet Kryvyi Rih, the rough industrial city in central Ukraine where Zelensky had grown up. The President reflected Ukraine not as some romantic idea, but as a reality: sometimes flawed and infuriating, but also benevolent and distinctive.

His approach to politics was also distinct from that of his predecessors. He did not exploit regional, linguistic differences in the way many earlier politicians had done. He exploited – if exploited is the right word – what people had in common, not what divided them. And what they had in common was resource-fulness, a desire for a normal life, and a rejection of the state and the old elites. If this was populism, then Zelensky was a populist.

I first met President Zelensky in June 2021. I inter-viewed him for *The Economist* in a vast reception room of the presidential administration office, built in 1936–9 – the period of Stalin's Great Terror – as the headquarters of Kyiv Military District. The building had housed the Nazi command during the war and later served as the main offices of the Central Com-mittee of the Ukrainian Communist Party. Taking up an entire block of central Kyiv, it was a physical manifestation of Stalin's regime and of the state's power over the individual.

Zelensky looked decidedly out of place. 'I still don't feel comfortable here,' he told me. The archi-tecture was the antithesis to his idea of Ukraine as a decentralised, non-hierarchical, democratic country. I was struck by his sincerity, his desire to transform Ukraine and his lack of a plan to do so. I struggled to find a compelling way to frame the article I was writ-ing. 'I have been impetuous in my drive for change, but I am not the kind of person who starts off with an exit strategy,' was one of his best quotes. He seemed out of his depth, taking on a system that would almost certainly demolish him. I could barely imagine him as a war leader.

The next time I met the President, the building had reverted to its original purpose: a military headquarters. It was late March 2022 and my editor, Zanny Minton Beddoes, and I had travelled to Kyiv by train. It was my first time in Ukraine since the start of the war and what we saw was reminiscent of a Second World War movie. Towns under curfew and train lights dimmed to avoid detection. The eerie silence in Lviv railway station, filled with people running from the war: women with sunken eyes, too exhausted to talk; children silent, too exhausted to cry. The sounds and sights of dislocated life – wailing air-raid sirens, tank traps dotting the deserted streets, Russian forces still on the outskirts of Kyiv.

'Welcome to our fortress,' was how armed men greeted us when we walked through the building's gate, now reinforced by sandbags. Zelensky no longer looked out of place as he emerged from the bunker, dug by the Soviets in case of an air raid and deep enough to withstand a nuclear bomb. But there was nothing Churchillian about his manner. The enormity of what was happening around him ruled out any possibility of role play. He spoke not like a commander-in-chief, but as an ordinary man thrust into extraordinary circumstances. He had also aged by about ten years and grown a beard.

Politicians rarely listen to an interviewer's question; more often they simply wait for you to stop talking before delivering a pre-rehearsed message. Zelensky was different: he listened, he thought, and he engaged in a conversation conducted in three languages. 'We are not heroes. We do our job, and we are where we are,' he said. It was clear that he was not commanding an army – the generals were doing that, and he was wise enough to leave them to it. Nor was he micromanaging mayors and local communities – they were closer to the action and had a better sense of how to organise things. Everyone in Ukraine was doing what they did best, and Zelensky was no exception: communicating with Ukrainians, lobbying governments and businesses to supply arms. This was a volunteer nation, and Zelensky was its volunteer-in-chief.

In his speeches to parliaments and assemblies around the world, Zelensky would address not only – or even primarily – politicians; he appealed to the people who elected them. Large pro-Ukrainian demonstrations in Berlin, Paris and London, galvanised by his addresses, compelled governments to go further in their support of Ukraine than anyone had thought was possible. These speeches resonated as strongly as they did, perhaps, because Zelensky delivered a message of such moral clarity and force that it left few people indifferent. His words contained something that people in the West – particularly of a younger generation – had been searching for: a sense of meaning in a post-ideological society in which liberty had long been taken for granted. The world had not heard words of such significance since the fall of the Berlin Wall and the so-called 'end of history'.

Vladimir Putin's genocidal war against Ukraine's identity, culture and people was a reminder that history was far from over, and that fascism – its greatest evil – was far from dead. But if Putin created this war, Zelensky narrated it. There is no distinction between the words 'history' and 'story' in either Ukrainian or Russian, and in his speeches Zelensky recounted both: the stories of individual people and a narrative of the most deadly European conflict since the end of the Second World War.

The speeches Zelensky has chosen to include in this book represent another attempt to tell that story. As winter gave way to spring, their references and examples would change, but Zelensky's message stayed the same. The war being fought in Ukraine was not a regional war for territory, or a struggle for geopolitical dominance. It was a war between a corrupt, nuclear state and a people who merely wished to live peacefully in their own land, in their own way. It was a war between empathy and hatred, between dignity and enslavement, and ultimately between life and death. Ukraine's war, Zelensky argued, was everybody's war.

When Putin began this war, the Russian armed forces reportedly packed their parade uniforms in their bags as they advanced towards the capital; soldiers expected to be welcomed with open arms and be parading in Kyiv within days. Six months later, on Ukraine's Independence Day, there were Russian tanks in the centre of Kyiv: burned out and mangled ones. This display of destroyed Russian armour was a parade of Ukraine's defiance, not to mention its sense of humour. And Zelensky's speech on that day – 24 August – marked a turning point. Ukraine no longer wanted peace with Russia, he said. It wanted victory.

At the time of writing, that victory no longer seems impossible. In the weeks after 24 August, Ukrainian forces staged a spectacular offensive, liberating more territory in a few days than Russia had managed to take in the previous five months. Putin, desperate and

humiliated, lashed out at Ukrainian civilian infrastructure and threatened a nuclear strike. Zelensky
responded with a post on social media: 'Read my lips:
Without gas or without you? Without you. Without
light or without you? Without you. Without water or
without you? Without you. Without food or without
you? Without you.'

The rhetorical power of Zelensky's address came
from the quality that has defined so many of his
speeches: truth. It has given Zelensky a singular
ability to shape how the world thinks about Ukraine.
Nobody can tell how long this war will continue or
how it will end, nor what kind of President Zelensky
will be when the fighting is over. But one thing seems
certain. If Putin's aim was to erase Ukraine, its state-
hood and its identity, he lost on the day of invasion.
As Zelensky put it in that first video, Ukraine is '*tut*'.
Here to stay.

Arkady Ostrovsky
October 2022

*Arkady Ostrovsky is an award-winning British author
and journalist. He is the Russia and Eastern Europe
Editor of* The Economist.

A MESSAGE FROM UKRAINE

Introduction:
To Change the Past

I would be the happiest person in the world if the book you are holding in your hands had never been published.

If my addresses after 24 February 2022 had never been written or spoken, and if my speeches after the invasion had never been heard or read.

I know that this is an abrupt way to begin my introduction. For the vast majority of books it would be too much. This book is the exception. I write these words not as an attempt to grab your attention, nor in a phoney stab at glory. The reason I need your attention is far too painful, the price of any 'glory' far too high. It is the war that has been unleashed against Ukraine. It is the thousands of lives taken by Russia.

If only we could change the past. There is so much I would give up in an instant. The acclaim and admiration from countries around the world. I would prefer that when people heard the surname Zelensky, they replied, 'Who?' I would rather I had never heard the applause of the US Congress, the British House of Commons or the European Parliament – and that Ukrainians had never heard the sound of explosions or gunshots in our homeland.

If only we could change the past. I would rather it wasn't my face on the cover of *TIME* magazine, but instead a doctor working on a cure for cancer; that lists of the world's most influential people focused not on politicians, but on the scientists finding ways to overcome hunger and global warming, chemical and biological warfare, even the nuclear threat facing the world.

If only we could change the past. I would give up every mention of my name in the global press, every repost on social media. At heart, I don't care about gaining new followers on Instagram and Facebook; all I feel is my heart breaking for the thousands killed in Bucha and Izyum – for all the dead Ukrainians.

Assuming you live on planet Earth, you probably already know what has been happening in Ukraine for the last eight years. Assuming that you are in your right mind – that you have a clear head and a caring heart – you already know the significance of

24 February 2022. Maybe you understand why writing 'rf' with lower-case letters is only fair.* Perhaps you even understand why the beginning of this introduction takes the form it does: abrupt, intense, jarring.

Such are the times in which it has been written. Such is the war in which these words have been uttered. You are right. In the vast majority of books, this opening would be too much. This book is the exception.

But this is not a book about how we are unable to change the past. It is a book about how we can build the future. And it is a book about how Ukraine and its people are already doing so.

This process did not start on 24 February. Ukraine did not appear on the world map in early 2022. Ukrainians were not born in the moment of the rf's invasion. We were, we are and we will be; we have existed, we exist, and we will continue to exist. And so, while we appreciate the help, support and attention the world has given us, the bravery of our people must not start being taken for granted. War must not become routine.

Do not forget about Ukraine. Do not get tired of Ukraine. Do not let our courage go 'out of fashion'.

* russian federation. The Ukrainian government does not capitalise the name of the Russian state, arguing that this would bestow it with undue political legitimacy.

Supporting Ukraine is not a trend, a meme or a viral challenge. It is not a force to rapidly spread across the planet and then just as rapidly disappear into oblivion. If you want to understand who we are and where we are from, what we want and where we are going, you must first learn more about us. This book will help you do just that.

***

We are not the ones who started this war. But we are the ones who must finish it. And we are ready for dialogue to do so.

What will bring the end of the war? We used to say 'peace'. Now we say 'victory'.

These words are taken from the first and last speeches that appear in this book. There are three years and three months between them: from 20 May 2019 through to 24 August 2022. This is the period of Ukrainian history I will lead you through. This is the path we have walked as a nation.

These words succinctly describe how I have changed, and so have my team and the Ukrainian people. We did not want war. We did everything we could to prevent war. I was uttering words to this effect from the first moments after I was sworn in as President until the final hours leading up to the Russian invasion.

Every time the rf lit a match over the powder keg, we extinguished it. We did not give in to their provocations, nor strike out when they violated every agreement our two countries had come to. We have always striven for peace, always been committed to the diplomatic solution, always asked for dialogue and for negotiations.

On 24 February at 4.30 a.m., we received the rf's answer. Their actions made it clear. They wanted to destroy Ukraine; to wipe us off the face of the Earth, both as a state and as a people.

Ukrainians had heard this answer before, of course. It has been uttered in many languages, across many ages, by many invaders. And the same end awaited them all. Ultimately, every invading army fled back across the border they had made the mistake of crossing. They abandoned their weapons and equipment, hurrying and limping from our country.

This is what the rf forces have done, too. They have cursed the day they crossed into our land and saw the kind and peaceful people of Ukraine turn into lions, ready to tear apart any enemy.

They have watched a friendly and hospitable people become warriors, offering them not the grain from our fields but the lead from our rifles.

They have witnessed students and scientists, musicians and actors, teachers and doctors, engineers and farmers come together with the military. To beat the world's second-strongest army, to send the flagship of the Russian fleet to the bottom of the ocean, to master the M270 MLRS and HIMARS in under a week – and to liberate thousands of kilometres of territory in just a few days.

Who are these Ukrainians? You will find answers in the sixteen speeches collected here. They have not been chosen at random. Since my inauguration in May 2019, I have delivered about a thousand different addresses around the world. I have selected the speeches in this book because, more than any others, they will help you understand us: our aspirations, our principles and our values.

In these pages, then, I invite you to learn about Ukraine. Learn about our dreams and about those who tried to shatter them. Discover what we were like before the invasion, how the war changed us, and why. Read about our lives and our history over the past three years.

Above all, hear our message: one that rang out loud and clear on Independence Day 2022, and will ring out until the last rf soldier leaves our territory. 'What will bring the end of the war? We used to say "peace". Now we say "victory".'

President Volodymyr Zelensky
October 2022

PART I
OUR VALUES

'Freedom is not about having unshackled hands. Freedom is about having unshackled minds.'

IN APRIL 2019, Volodymyr Zelensky was elected President of Ukraine. Over the previous four months, the former TV producer and comedian had fought a campaign that emphasised his outsider status and his determination to take on Ukraine's old political elite. Now, he had the chance to remake the country. Ukraine, Zelensky said in his inauguration address, was on the verge of entering 'a new era', defined by a new set of values. In the years that followed, Zelensky would outline his vision for that era everywhere from the Ukrainian Parliament to the rostrum of the UN Security Council. He would describe Ukraine as a democratic, independent nation, free of corruption and confident of its place at the heart of Europe. Zelensky also outlined the greatest threat to this new era: Russia. Vladimir Putin, Zelensky argued, could not bear the choice the Ukrainian people had made: Europe over Russia, and democracy over autocracy.

2

'We Are All the President Now'

Inaugural address to the Ukrainian Parliament
Kyiv, 20 May 2019

After I was elected, my six-year-old son said, 'Dad, they say on TV that Zelensky is the President. Does that mean I'm the President too?'

At the time it sounded funny, but later I realised that it was true. Because each of us is the President. Not just the 73 per cent who voted for me, but all 100 per cent of Ukrainians. This is not just my victory; it is our common victory. And it is a common opportunity for which we are all responsible.

Because it isn't just me who has taken the oath. Every one of us has just put a hand on the Constitution and sworn allegiance to Ukraine.

Now, imagine the headlines if that were the case. 'The President Does Not Pay His Taxes'. 'The President Ran a Red Light While Drunk'. Or perhaps, 'The

President is Quietly Stealing Because that's What Everyone Else Does'. Wouldn't that be shameful? This is what I mean when I say that each of us is the President. Building Ukraine is a responsibility we all share. From now on, it is down to all of us to create the country that we want to leave to our children.

For if we are to be a European country, that Europeanness begins with each one of us. We have chosen a path that leads to Europe, but Europe is not somewhere 'out there'. Europe is here, in the mind. And after it appears there, it will appear everywhere in Ukraine.

That is our common dream. But we also share a common pain. Each of us has died in Donbas. Each of us is a refugee. Each of us is a migrant worker. And each of us is the one living in poverty.

But we will get through it. Because each of us is also a Ukrainian.

There are no greater or lesser citizens of this nation. From Uzhhorod to Luhansk, Chernihiv to Simferopol, Lviv to Kharkiv, Donetsk to Dnipro to Odesa, we are all Ukrainians. And we must stand as one. For we are only strong when we are united.

So today, I appeal to Ukrainians all around the world. There are 65 million of us. Ukrainians in Europe and Asia, in North and South America,

Australia and Africa – I appeal to you all. We need you. I will gladly grant citizenship to anyone who is ready to build a new, strong and successful Ukraine. Come not to visit, but to return home. Don't come bearing souvenirs from abroad; simply bring your knowledge, experience and values.

This will in turn help us start a new era. Sceptics will say this is impossible, a fantasy. But what if that is precisely what defines us as a nation: to unite and achieve the impossible, against all odds?

Some of you will remember when the Icelandic soccer team qualified for the 2016 European Championship. A dentist, a director, a pilot, a student and a cleaner all came together to defend their country's pride. No one believed they could do it, but they did.

This should be our path too. We must become the Icelanders in soccer, the Israelis in the defence of their land, the Japanese in technology, and the Swiss in their ability to live together in harmony.

Our first task, though, is to achieve a ceasefire in Donbas. I have often been asked, What price are you prepared to pay for the ceasefire? It's a strange question. What price are you ready to pay for the lives of your loved ones? I am ready to pay any price to stop the deaths of our heroes. I am ready to give up my fame, my poll ratings – if need be, my position. The only thing I will not give up is our territory.

History is unfair. We are not the ones who started this war. But we are the ones who must finish it. And we are ready for dialogue to do so.

The first step will be the return of all Ukrainian prisoners. Our next step will be securing the 'return' of the lost territories. This term does not seem entirely correct to me, because it is impossible to return what has always been ours. Both Crimea and Donbas are Ukrainian land.

But it is land where we have lost the most important thing: the minds of the people who live there. And we need to win them back. Over the years, the authorities have done nothing to make the people of Crimea and Donbas feel like Ukrainians; to understand that they are not strangers, but our people.

Even if they were granted ten different passports from ten different countries, that fact wouldn't change. Being Ukrainian is not a line in the passport. Being Ukrainian is here, in the heart.

2

'Someone Else's War'

Address to the UN General Assembly
New York, 25 September 2019

Every person in this hall has a different set of values and a different set of problems. But there is one thing that unites you all. Each of you once delivered your first speech from this rostrum.

Please recall how you felt in that moment. Every one of you, so respected and honoured today, was once a 'beginner' at being a global politician. Since then, the cocktail of pragmatism, scepticism and harsh geopolitical reality that defines our world has still not quenched your passion; your unwavering belief that the world can be changed for the better.

Remember how important it was to communicate the troubles of your country and your people to the world on that day. Remember how important it was to be heard. That is how I feel today.

Let me tell you a story. It is the story of a person for whom 'being heard' was what gave life meaning. This man had a divine voice. He was hailed as one of the best baritones and countertenors in the world. His voice was heard at Carnegie Hall in New York, Notre-Dame Cathedral, Covent Garden in London and the Grand Opera in Paris. Each of you might have had the chance to hear his incredible singing.

But there is something that means you will not be able to. Let me show you, it looks like this.* 12.7 millimetres that ended not only his career, but his life. It costs ten dollars. Today, that is the value of a human life.

There are thousands such stories, millions such bullets. Welcome to the twenty-first century. This was supposed to be a century of opportunity; except today, instead of the opportunity to be heard, you have the opportunity to be killed.

This man was called Wassyl Slipak. He was a Ukrainian, a soloist at the Paris National Opera. And he was killed in Donbas while defending Ukraine from Russian aggression.

The war in Donbas has already lasted five years. Russia's annexation of the Ukrainian peninsula of

---

* Holding up a bullet.

Crimea has lasted five years too. Yet despite the requirements of international law and the hundreds of organisations designed to defend it, it is our country that must protect its sovereignty and territorial integrity. It is our country fighting with weapons in hand, losing its citizens.

More than 13,000 have been killed. Thirty thousand have been wounded. One and a half million people have been forced to leave their homes. Every year these horrific numbers are recited here, except with one change: they keep getting bigger.

My objectives are the end of the war, the return of all the occupied Ukrainian territories and the outbreak of peace. But not at the cost of our citizens' lives, nor at the cost of freedom, nor at the cost of Ukraine's right to choose its own path. That is why we need the support of the world.

Now, I understand that everyone present here has their own state's concerns at heart; and other people's problems should not worry you more than your own.

But what is happening in my country is no longer 'someone else's war'.

None of you can feel safe when there is a war in Ukraine. Not when there is a war in Europe.

It would be fatal to think that the situation in our country does not concern you and will never affect you. When you look at the world from a global perspective, you cannot avert your eyes from such 'details'. That outlook is what laid the foundation of the two world wars. Tens of millions of human lives were the cost of inattention, silence, inaction, or the unwillingness to sacrifice one's own ambitions for the greater good. Has humanity begun to forget these dreadful lessons of history?

Ukraine remembers them. Ukraine has always demonstrated its willingness to move towards peace in a civilised way, and take steps to enhance international security. Consider when Ukraine gave up its nuclear capability, which at the time was larger than that of the UK, France and China combined.*

Because we believed we were building a different world. A new world. A world in which you do not need to have a nuclear weapon to be heard. A world in which you are respected not for the number of warheads you hold, but for your actions.

Yet in this new world, our country has lost part of its territory and is losing its citizens almost every day. If Ukraine does not have the right to speak

* In the Budapest Memorandum of 1994, Ukraine agreed to relinquish its Soviet nuclear arsenal in return for assurances that Russia, the US and the UK would respect its sovereignty.

about the need to rethink the rules of this world, who does?

Of course, we do not question the authority of international institutions, particularly the United Nations. But we must admit that their mechanisms are not flawless . . . Let's be honest: Are nations really united today? If so, what exactly unites them? Disasters and wars, perhaps.

From this, the highest platform in the world, we hear constant calls for a fairer planet, promises of justice, and the announcement of new initiatives. It is time to make sure that they are backed by deeds. Because in today's world, where a human life costs ten dollars, words have long since lost their value.

Remember the goal behind the UN's establishment in 1945: to maintain and strengthen peace and international security. How do we respond when the very basis of international security is at stake?

Because any war today – whether in Ukraine, Syria, Libya, Yemen or any other corner of the planet – represents a grave threat to the whole of civilisation, regardless of its number of casualties. These wars show that in 2019, *Homo sapiens* still resolves conflicts with killing. For as long as humanity has existed, it has been finding new ways to travel ever greater distances, exchange information and cure diseases.

Only one thing has remained unchanged: that disputes between nations continue to be resolved not by debate, but by missiles. Not by words, but by war.

Do not allow yourself to believe that war is far away. Military methods, technologies and weapons mean that our planet is not as large as it once was. The time it has taken me to utter this paragraph would be long enough to destroy the Earth completely.

This means that every leader is responsible not only for the fate of their own country, but for the fate of the whole world. We must all realise that the strong leader is not the one who sends thousands of soldiers to their deaths without batting an eyelid. A strong leader is the one who protects the lives of everyone.

Let us ask ourselves a question. What do our meetings in this hall offer humanity, if for some it is nothing more than political theatre? If this room becomes a stage where we declare good intentions that are cancelled out by bad actions?

At this rostrum, we are not just enacting a scene from some play. The seven and a half billion inhabitants of the planet are not merely spectators, they are direct participants. The basic facts of the lives they lead are determined here. Indeed, whether or not they will have lives at all depends upon everyone here.

One day, I would like this speech to be known as the 'fifteen minutes that changed the world'. I am well aware, however, that changing something that has existed for thousands of years is impossible in fifteen minutes. Most behavioural theories tell us that war is an integral part of human nature.

But the world is changing, and people are changing with it. As the species that discovered writing and mathematics, invented the wheel and penicillin, and conquered space, humanity still has a chance. Being aware of the danger in which civilisation finds itself, we must generate other ways of living. We must fight for a new mentality in which aggression, anger and hatred are obsolete.

Ladies and gentlemen, on this day in 1970 Erich Maria Remarque died. Ninety years ago saw the publication of his novel *All Quiet on the Western Front*. Recall these words from its preface: that it would 'try simply to tell of a generation of men who, even though they may have escaped its shells, were destroyed by the war'. The same year also saw the publication of Ernest Hemingway's *A Farewell to Arms*. He wrote: 'War is not won by victory.' His point was that even the winner of a war never truly stops fighting.

The world must remember that every generation destroyed by war paves the path to the next one: a new war, which in turn will be impossible to win through victory alone. Today, people often say that if there is a Third World War, it will be the last. I hope this statement is a recognition of the dangers our planet faces, rather than a prediction of our future.

3

'The Opposite of Love'

Address to the United States Holocaust
Memorial Museum
Washington DC, 1 September 2021

The Second World War began eighty-two years ago
today, on 1 September 1939. It was the consequence
of an especially human cruelty; or rather an especially
inhuman hatred.

Its name was Nazism. Eighty-two years ago, it
tried to enslave humanity and take over the world.

Nazism has many connotations. Death. Famine.
Captivity. Bombed cities. Burned villages. Cremated people. *Ostarbeiter*.* Concentration camps.
The Holocaust.

At least 6 million Jews were the victims of Nazism

---

* Central and Eastern European slave workers forced to work
in Nazi Germany during the Second World War.

in Europe. One and a half million — one in four — were from Ukraine. And among them there was one family whose story I would like to tell.

It is a story about four brothers. Three of them were shot by the German invaders who attacked Ukraine, along with their parents, wives, children and all other relatives. The fourth brother survived. At the time of their murder he was away fighting at the front. He fought until the end of the Second World War, contributing to the victory over Nazism.

He would return home four years later. Two years after that, he had a son. Thirty-one years after that, his grandson was born. Then, forty years after that, his grandson became the President of Ukraine. He is standing in front of you.

Nazism was defeated, irrevocably and for ever. But it crippled many people's lives, and touched almost every family. However, along with those who gave their lives in the fight against Nazism, in almost every family are those who survived the fight against it.

They were able to pass on its memory to future generations. So that we could say, 'Never again.' So that we could prevent Nazism from ever coming back.

Tragically, supporters of the ideas of Nazism — of xenophobia and of inequality — still exist. They are present in many different countries and in many different forms. But their influence in modern Ukraine is less than zero. In Ukraine, racism and intolerance stand less than no chance.

Just look at Ukrainians' response to the propaganda of those who call our people Nazis and anti-Semites.* They elected me President.

Questions about the place of racism in Ukraine have been answered many times before. At least 2,659 times, in fact. That is how many Ukrainians officially bear the honorary title of 'Righteous Among the Nations': people who saved Jews, often at the cost of their own lives.† Ukraine is the fourth country on the list. As President, I have established lifelong pensions for the Ukrainian citizens who saved Jews during the Holocaust. It is the least the state can do today to honour their courage and self-sacrifice.

Ukrainian minds will bear no trace of anti-Semitism and Nazism. These evils have no place in the hearts of the people who survived Babyn Yar.

Last year, on Holocaust Memorial Day, we opened

---

* The Kremlin has stated that one of the objectives of its 'special military operation' was to 'denazify' Ukraine.
† Honorific title used by the State of Israel to refer to non-Jews who saved the lives of Holocaust victims.

a memorial in the middle of Kyiv. Inside, there are photos from the time of the Nazi occupation of Kyiv. One photo shows a group of people walking past two Jews who have been killed.

It is a terrible but necessary symbol for future generations. It shows that these evil crimes become possible when people choose not to notice. To keep silent. To walk past. It is a truth that Ukrainians have not forgotten.

Nor have we forgotten the short, cold, cruel announcement posted in Kyiv by the Nazi occupiers. 'It is ordered that all the Jews of the city of Kyiv and its surroundings gather on Monday, 29 September 1941, before 8 o'clock in the morning, at Melnyka-Dehtyarivska Street, near the cemetery. Everyone should take documents, money, underwear, etc. with them.'

Two sentences. A few dozen words. And hundreds of thousands killed.

Over the next two days, the Nazis killed almost 34,000 people in Babyn Yar. Over the next two years, according to some estimates, they would kill up to 200,000 there.

It is our duty to commemorate the victims' memory. But for a long time, there was no such commemoration. In Soviet times, a sports complex and a shooting range were built on the site of the massacre. From 1991 onwards, Babyn Yar was bulldozed, rather than memorialised. Over the last two years, we have been changing that. At the end of 2020, I signed the decree 'On Measures for the Further Development of the National Historical and Memorial Reserve Babyn Yar'. It goes some way to correct the historical failure to honour Babyn Yar's victims.

I have been reflecting on the age at which it is appropriate to take one's son to this memorial. Is now too early? And then I remembered the story of an eight-year-old girl who survived Auschwitz. She talked about the forced labour in the workshop where Nazi bombs and shells were sorted. Boxes that were identified as defective were marked with a white cross. She erased the marks on some of these boxes. If anyone had noticed, she would have been shot on the spot. But she did it anyway. And of the thousands of bombs that the Nazis dropped on cities and villages, some did not explode.

How many lives did she save? We don't know for sure. But her story does teach us that it can never be 'too early' to tell children what the Holocaust is, what Nazism is, and why it must never happen again.

In less than a month, on 29 September, we will mark the eightieth anniversary of the beginning of the mass shootings in Babyn Yar. We will honour the memory of the victims during the week leading up to 6 October. I would like to invite you, together with your children and grandchildren, to Ukraine and to Kyiv – so that together we can pray for the souls of all those who died at the site and during the Holocaust.

We do so with deep respect for the memory of generations past, and with unwavering faith in peace for those to come.

For Ukrainians will always honour the memory of the victims of the Shoah. Our hearts can fully understand this tragedy, because we ourselves experienced a great tragedy: the famine-genocide.* It is not something you can turn away from.

In the same way, you cannot turn away from the tragedy we are experiencing today: the war in Donbas, in which Ukrainian citizens are dying. Ukrainians who are Orthodox Christians, Jews, Catholics, Muslims and of many other faiths.

Today, cities in Eastern Ukraine, liberated from

---

* A reference to the Holodomor or Great Famine of 1932–3. The famine, induced by Stalin's policy of collectivisation, killed millions of Ukrainian peasants, and many historians believe it amounted to genocide.

the Nazis eighty years ago, have two occupations they must commemorate.

Today, children and grandchildren tell their grandparents about war, and not the other way around.

Today, Ukraine is in a state of war. You can't forget about it. You can't ignore it.

You must not think that this concerns only Ukraine and Russia . . . For Nazism begins with the violation of international law, with the violation of human rights, with murders and imprisonments. Elie Wiesel, the Nobel Laureate and survivor of Auschwitz and Buchenwald, said, 'The opposite of love is not hate. It is indifference.'

Do not be indifferent to the war in Donbas or to the occupation of Crimea. Do not be indifferent to Ukraine.

4

'Invincible'

Address on the Day of Dignity and Freedom
Kyiv, 21 November 2021

We are a free people, free to create our own future. We should be proud of that. For we have paid – and continue to pay – a high price for our freedom.

We will never forget all those who have given their lives for Ukraine. We will never forgive those who took their lives and sought to deprive us of our freedom. And we will never stop feeling pride that they did not succeed – and that they never will.

For now is the time to change the way we think of ourselves. Ukrainians are not victims; nor are we oppressed, or divided, or captive. We are beautiful, strong, brave, intelligent, talented. We are invincible.

And we are invincible because we have our dignity. Ukrainians understand a simple truth: that a life without freedom is no life at all. We know that to lose our freedom would be to lose our honour. To lose our honour would be to lose our hearts. To lose our hearts would be to lose our souls. And to lose our souls would be to lose our lives.

That is why we fight for freedom, even at the cost of our own lives. Because we are fighting *for* our lives.

Dignity and freedom. For Ukrainians, these words have long been imbued with a deep meaning. I will never forget a story some Ukrainian sailors told upon returning home from captivity. They were prisoners, but they remained free in spirit. They joked so loudly that their jailers told them to be quiet; usually this was a place where people cried, but they wouldn't stop laughing. As they were transported across the country, they sat in a wagon and sang the national anthem . . . These Ukrainians did not behave like captives, because they had not lost their dignity. They proved that in a foreign land – even in prison – you can still be free.

Because freedom is not about having unshackled hands. Freedom is about having unshackled minds.

Take Vasyl Stus.* After the Soviet authorities unleashed a wave of arrests of creative young people

* Ukrainian poet and dissident (1938–85).

across Ukraine, he rose to his feet at the premiere of Sergei Parajanov's film *Shadows of Forgotten Ancestors* and said, 'Everyone who opposes the arrests, stand up.' A few people got up. Then more. And then even more.

Why would Stus stage such a protest? He knew that by doing so, he might lose his freedom. But he knew that if he didn't, he would certainly lose his dignity.

Or take Omelyan Kovch, the priest who rescued Jews during the Holocaust by giving them baptismal records that said they were Christians. For this he was sent to the Majdanek concentration camp. He lost his freedom for ever, but he never lost his dignity.

In a letter home, he apologised for choosing to stay even after he was offered early release. 'These people need me here,' he wrote. 'They think they will die soon, and so they come to me for confession. If I go, they will be left without hope. They have already been deprived of dignity, honour, freedom; their homes, relatives, names; they will soon be deprived of their lives. I will not take away their hope.'

Or take Leonid Bykov.* He did not give up his principles or his creative freedom. He wanted to

* Soviet Ukrainian actor and film director (1928–79).

film his masterpiece, *Only 'Old Men' Are Going into Battle*, in colour; but the authorities would only give him black-and-white film. Did this hurt his dignity? Maybe. But did he lose it? No. And he made a black-and-white film that is adored by millions – a film about people who are dignified and free.

Like those who stood on Maidan Square in the uprisings of 1990, 2004 and 2014. Like those who hold the line in the trenches in the east of Ukraine, defending our state.

They are all different. They fight wearing the cross, the crescent, the Star of David. Lads from Western Ukraine and from the south-east. Russian speakers from Kharkiv and Kryvyi Rih and Ukrainian speakers from Ternopil and Ivano-Frankivsk. People from Cherkasy, Vinnytsia, Mykolaiv; from Kyiv, from Donbas, from Luhansk, from Crimea.

All different. All Ukrainians. All our champions. They know that dignity is something you must never give up defending. But Ukrainians are not used to giving up. And that is why we Ukrainians have our freedom.

PART II
OUR FIGHT

'We are strong. We are ready for everything. We will defeat anyone. Because we are Ukraine.'

AT 4.30 A.M. on 24 February 2022, the Russian army crossed into Ukraine. Over the previous year, Vladimir Putin had amassed well over 100,000 troops on the country's border, demanding that it surrender its sovereignty and give up on its choice to move towards the West. Many assumed that the Ukrainian military, massively outnumbered by the Russian aggressors, would buckle – and that the regime in Kyiv would collapse. But the war did not play out how Putin had expected. In the days and weeks that followed, Ukraine fought back. And so did Zelensky. Far from fleeing the country, the President stayed in Kyiv and took on a new role: delivering daily addresses that powerfully captured the resilience and strength of the Ukrainian people.

5

'The Lessons of History'

Speech to the Munich Security Conference
Munich, 19 February 2022

Two days ago I was in Donbas, on the demarcation line.

Officially, it marks the line between Ukraine and the temporarily occupied territories. In fact, it marks the line between peace and war. On one side there is a kindergarten, on the other a bomb crater. On one side there is a school, on the other a playground destroyed by a missile.

And in the school on the occupied side there are thirty children who still go there to learn.

Some have physics classes. Knowing the basic laws of physics, even these children understand the absurdity of the claim that the shelling is carried out by Ukraine.

Some have maths classes. Even without a calculator,

these children can calculate the difference between the number of times they have been attacked in these last three days and the number of times Ukraine is mentioned in this year's Munich Security Report.*

And some have history classes. So, when a bomb crater appears in their school grounds, these children have a question: Has the world forgotten the mistakes of the twentieth century?

Where do attempts at appeasement lead? these children ask. They remember the French anti-war slogan, 'Why die for Danzig?' – how it led to the need to die for Dunkirk and dozens of other cities in Europe and around the world. They remember how appeasement cost tens of millions of lives.

These are the lessons of history. We have all read the same books. And so, surely, we all understand that we face some grave questions.

How did it happen that, in the twenty-first century, Europe is again at war and people are dying?

How is it that this conflict has lasted longer than the Second World War?

How did we get to the biggest security crisis since the Cold War?

---

* The 2022 report dedicated one of its seven chapters to security in Eastern Europe.

As the President of a country that has lost part of its territory, thousands of people, and on whose borders there are now 150,000 Russian troops as well as equipment and heavy weapons, to me the answer is obvious.

The architecture of world security is fragile and needs to be updated. The rules that the world agreed upon decades ago no longer work. They do not keep up with new threats, and they are not effective in overcoming them. They offer a cough syrup when what you need is a Covid vaccine.

The security system is fragile. It crashes, and crashes again. There are many reasons: selfishness, arrogance, the irresponsibility of states at a global level. As a result, we have crimes from some and indifference from others. Indifference that leads to complicity.

It is symbolic that I am talking about this at the Munich Security Conference. It was here, fifteen years ago, that Russia announced its intention to challenge the global security order.

How did the world respond? Appeasement.

What was the result? The annexation of Crimea and aggression against my state.

The United Nations, which is supposed to defend peace and world security, cannot defend itself. When its charter is violated. When one of the members of the Security Council annexes the territory of one of the UN's founding members. And when the UN itself ignores the Crimea Platform,* the goal of which is to end the occupation peacefully and protect the rights of Crimeans.

Three years ago, it was here that Angela Merkel said, 'Who will pick up the wreckage of the world order? Only all of us, together.' The audience gave her a standing ovation. But the collective applause did not grow into collective action. And now, when the world is talking about the threat of a great war, the question arises: Is there anything left to pick up? The security architecture in Europe and the world is almost destroyed.

It is too late to think about repairs. It is time to build a new system.

Humankind has been here twice before, and paid too high a price: two world wars. Now, we have a chance to reverse this trend before it becomes a consistent pattern. That means building a different system, before there are millions of victims. With the lessons of the First and Second World Wars in mind, let us not, God forbid, experience a third.

---

* Ukrainian diplomatic summit attempting to reverse the Russian annexation of Crimea.

Here, and on the rostrum of the UN, I have talked about how in the twenty-first century there is no such thing as a 'foreign' war. That means everyone must take the situation in Ukraine seriously. It means realising that the annexation of Crimea and the war in Donbas affect everyone across the globe. And it means recognising that this is not just a war in Ukraine, but a war in Europe.

I said this at summits and forums in 2019, 2020, 2021. Will the world be able to hear me in 2022?

The world is waking up to this threat, but it is not yet fully awake. We need more action, not just tweets and headlines. And the rest of the world needs this as much as Ukraine does.

We will defend our land with or without the support of partners. We appreciate any help, whether it is hundreds of modern weapons or 5,000 helmets. But everyone should understand that these are not charitable contributions that Ukraine is asking for, nor noble gestures for which Ukraine should bow low in thanks. This is your contribution to the security of Europe and the world.

A world in which Ukraine has been your reliable shield for eight years. A world in which for nearly a decade we have been rebuffing one of the world's biggest armies.

Today that army stands along our borders, not the borders of the EU. Grad rockets hit Mariupol, not European cities. After almost six months of fighting, it was Donetsk airport that was destroyed, not Frankfurt. And in the last few days, the real heat has been felt in the Avdiivka Industrial Zone, not in Montmartre.

No EU country knows what it means to have military burials every day in every region. And no other European leader knows what it means to hold regular meetings with the families of the deceased.

Nevertheless, we will defend our beautiful land – no matter if we have 50,000, 150,000 or 1 million soldiers on the border. To really help Ukraine, it is not necessary to obsess over the number of Russian servicemen and how much military equipment is on the border. Focus instead on how many of us there are.

We will defend our land whether invasion comes on 16 February, 1 March or 31 December. To really help Ukraine, it is not helpful to talk only about the timeline of the probable invasion. We need other timelines much more, and everyone in this room understands perfectly well which ones.

Tomorrow in Ukraine is the Day of the Heroes of

the Heavenly Hundred.* Eight years ago, Ukrainians made their choice; many gave their lives for it. Eight years later, why must Ukraine constantly call for the EU to recognise its movement towards membership?

Since 2014, Russia has been trying to convince Ukraine that we have chosen the wrong path, that no help is coming from Europe. Why won't Europe prove them wrong? Why won't the EU say today that its citizens are positive about Ukraine's accession? Doesn't Ukraine deserve direct and honest answers? The same question applies to NATO. The door is open, we are told. But so far, entry is still forbidden to some.

If not all members of the Alliance want to acknowledge us, be honest. Open doors are good. But today, above all, we need open answers.

* Ukrainian national day commemorating over a hundred people who died in the democratic revolution of 2014.

6

'Do Russians Want War?'

Address to the Ukrainian and Russian people
Kyiv, 24 February 2022, 12.30 a.m.

Ukrainians, I will be speaking briefly and sincerely. Today, we have strengthened the defence capabilities and resilience of our state. To support the soldiers who are protecting us, we have introduced a state of emergency for thirty days across the whole of Ukraine. This decision was supported by 335 deputies of the Parliament. A great defensive coalition has begun its work.

Parliament also adopted a package of measures to finance the defence sector. Tomorrow, the deputies will go to the regions to support our people. Our international partners are mobilised to support Ukraine . . . And I have also met with the representatives of major Ukrainian businesses. They all remain in Ukraine along with their teams, and are working to protect the country. Thank you to everyone who is helping Ukraine. Let us keep working.

And now, in Russian.* Today, I attempted to call the President of the russian federation. I was met with silence. In a just world, the silence would be in Donbas.

So today I want to appeal to all the citizens of Russia – not as President, but as a citizen of Ukraine.

We are separated by more than 2,000 kilometres of shared border. Today, your forces stand along that border; almost 200,000 soldiers and thousands of military vehicles. Your leaders have given approval for them to step into the territory of another country. This step could mark the beginning of a huge war on the European continent.

Today, the whole world is talking about what will happen next. Any provocation – any spark – could burn everything to the ground. You are told that this flame will bring freedom to the people of Ukraine. But the Ukrainian people are already free. We remember our past, and we are building our future ourselves: building it, not destroying it, in spite of what you are told every day on the television.

* From here onwards, Zelensky speaks in Russian.

The Ukraine in your news and the Ukraine in real life are two completely different countries. And the main difference is that ours exists.

You are told that we are Nazis. How can a country that gave more than 8 million lives in the struggle against Nazism support Nazism? How could I be a Nazi? Tell that to my grandfather. He went through the entire war fighting as an infantryman for the Soviet Army, and died as a colonel in independent Ukraine.

You are told that we hate Russian culture. How is it possible to hate a culture? Neighbours always enrich one another culturally. But that does not make us a single entity; it does not dissolve us into you. We are different. But that is no reason to be enemies. We merely want to create our history ourselves: peacefully, calmly, honestly.

You are told that I will order an attack on Donbas, to shoot and bomb indiscriminately. But this raises some very simple questions. Shoot at whom? Bomb what? Donetsk, a city I have visited dozens of times and looked people in the eye? Artyom Street, where I have walked with friends? Donbas Arena, where I rooted for the Ukrainian team at the Euros in 2012 with the locals? Scherbakova Park, where we drank together when our guys lost? Luhansk, where my best friend's mother lives? The site where my best friend's father is buried?

I am saying these words in Russian. But note that nobody in Russia knows what I am talking about. These places, these streets, these names, these events — they are all alien to you.

We fight because this is *our* land. This is *our* history. What will *you* fight for?

Many of you have been to Ukraine. Many of you have relatives in Ukraine. Some of you studied in Ukrainian universities, and befriended Ukrainian people.

You know our character. You know our people. You know our principles. You know what we value. So please listen to yourselves. Listen to the voice of reason: to common sense.

Hear us. The people of Ukraine want peace. The Ukrainian authorities want peace. We want it, and we will do everything we can to build it.

We are not alone. Many countries support Ukraine. Why? Because we are not talking about peace at any cost. We are talking about both peace and principles. We are talking about justice and about international law. About the right to self-determination, the right to decide our own future, the right to security, and the right to live without being threatened.

All these are important to us. They are important to the rest of the world. And I know for certain that they are important to you too.

We know one thing above all. We don't need war – neither cold, nor hot, nor hybrid. But if we come under attack – if someone tries to take away our country, our freedom, our lives, the lives of our children – we will defend ourselves. And as you attack us, you will see our faces, not our backs.

War is a calamity that carries a huge cost. People lose their money, their reputation, their quality of life. They lose their freedom. But most importantly, they lose their loved ones – and they lose themselves. There is a lack of everything good, and an abundance of pain, filth, blood and death. There are thousands – tens of thousands – of dead.

You say that Ukraine could present a threat to Russia. This was not the case in the past, is not the case now, and will not be the case in the future. You demand security guarantees from NATO. And we demand guarantees for Ukraine's security: guarantees from you, from Russia, and from the other guarantors of the Budapest Memorandum.

Today, we find ourselves outside of any defensive alliances. But the security of Ukraine is connected to the security of our neighbours. That is why it is necessary to talk about the security of all of Europe.

But our main goal is peace in Ukraine and the safety of Ukrainians. To achieve this goal, we are prepared to have a dialogue with anyone – including with you – in any form and in any forum.

War deprives everyone of 'guarantees'. Security, after all, will no longer be guaranteed for anyone.

Who will suffer the most from this? The people.

Who does not want it more than anyone? The people.

Who can prevent it? The people.

Are such people present among you? I am sure they are. Public figures, journalists, musicians, actors, athletes, scientists, doctors, bloggers, stand-up comedians, social media influencers and more. Men, women, the elderly, children, fathers, and most importantly, mothers.

Just like the people in Ukraine. Just like the authorities in Ukraine, no matter how much they try to convince you otherwise.

I know they will not show this appeal on Russian television. But the citizens of Russia must see it. They must know the truth. And the truth is that this situation needs to end before it is too late.

If the Russian leadership does not want to sit around a table with us for the sake of peace, then perhaps they will sit down with you.

Do Russians want war? I would like to answer this question myself. But the answer depends only on you, the citizens of the russian federation.

7

'We Are Ukraine'

Address to the Ukrainian people
Kyiv, 24 February 2022, 6 a.m.

Dear Ukrainian citizens, this morning, President Putin announced a special military operation in Donbas. Russia has carried out strikes on our military infrastructure and our border guard divisions. Explosions have been heard in many Ukrainian cities. We have introduced martial law across the country.

I have just had a phone call with President Biden. The United States of America has already started to gather international support for our cause.

Today, we need each of you to remain calm. If you can, please stay at home.

We are all working to protect the country. The army is working. The whole security and defence sector is working.

I will be in constant contact with you. So will the

National Security and Defence Council of Ukraine, and the Cabinet Ministers of Ukraine.

I will talk to you again soon. Do not panic. We are strong. We are ready for everything. We will defeat anyone. Because we are Ukraine.

Glory to Ukraine.

8

'A War Against Europe'

Address to the people of Europe
Kyiv, 25 February 2022

Yesterday the Chancellor of Germany, Olaf Scholz, said that Russia's invasion of Ukraine is something Europe has not witnessed for seventy-five years. And that is true. But it is not the whole truth.

This is not merely Russia's invasion of Ukraine. It is the beginning of a war against Europe. A war against the unity of Europe, against elementary human rights in Europe, against the peaceful co-existence of the countries of Europe — and against the fact that European states refuse to settle border disputes by force.

The cities of Ukraine are being bombed for a second day. Europe has seen tank columns and air strikes before, during the Second World War. We once said, 'Never again.' But here we are again — now, in 2022, over seventy-five years after the Second World War ended.

I know that Europe can see this. But what we do not see – at least not fully – is what you are going to do about it. How are you going to protect yourselves when you have been so slow to protect Ukraine?

We are grateful for what has been done already. The United States, Canada, the United Kingdom, the European Union, Australia and New Zealand have introduced sectoral sanctions against Russia – namely against the largest Russian banks and businesses, and against Russia's access to Western technologies.

But Russian tanks are still shooting at residential buildings in our cities. Armoured vehicles are still attacking our civilians. Europe has sufficient force to stop this aggression. What more will Europe do?

Will you cancel visas for Russians? Cut Russia off from SWIFT?* How about recalling ambassadors? Agreeing to an oil embargo? Imposing a no-fly zone? All of these should be on the table. Because Russia is a threat to all of us; to all of Europe.

You can still stop the aggression. But you must act without delay.

---

* The international payments system used by most banks globally.

Ordinary people in every country of the world can also do their part. Go out on the squares of your cities and demand peace for Ukraine – demand peace for Europe. It is our right, and it is your right.

When bombs fall in Kyiv, they fall in Europe. When missiles kill Ukrainians, they kill Europeans. More protection for Ukraine means more protection for Europe, and more protection for the democratic world.

The states of Europe are in no hurry to make strong decisions. But every European who resides in their capital can contribute. Go to the Ukrainian embassy and offer to help. Demand that your government gives more financial and military assistance to Ukraine. This not only helps us, it also helps you. For it helps Europe itself.

If you are a European with combat experience and do not want to sit idly by watching the indecision of politicians, come to Ukraine; come to protect Europe. Your help is urgently required.

Europeans, you have already been blackmailed with natural gas. You have already been humiliated. Russia wants to play divide and rule with Europe, just as they are trying to divide and rule Ukraine today.

Protect yourselves. Just as we protect ourselves.

PART III
OUR VOICE

'Today, it is not enough to be the leader of the nation. Today, it is necessary to be the leader of the world.'

WITH HIS SPEECH to the UK Parliament on 8 March 2022, Volodymyr Zelensky opened a new front in Ukraine's war with Russia: a war of communication. Over the next six months, President Zelensky would deliver over a hundred speeches to audiences around the world. While the content of each speech was different, the message was always the same. Everywhere from the US Congress to the Israeli Knesset, Zelensky emphasised the need for the world to offer military aid to Ukraine and impose sanctions on Russia; to support democracy and stand up for freedom. Along the way, Zelensky would give the Ukrainian people a voice on the world stage.

9

'Ukraine Did Not Seek Greatness. But Ukraine Has Become Great'

Address to the UK Parliament
London (via video link), 8 March 2022

Today I address all the people of the United Kingdom. You are a great people, with a great history. I speak to you as a citizen – and as President – of another great country: a great country with a dream.

I want to tell you about the last thirteen days of our war. It is a war we did not start and did not want, but a war we are waging. Because we do not want to lose what is ours: Ukraine. Just as you did not want to lose what was yours when the Nazis tried to invade, and you had to fight for Britain.

On the first day, cruise missiles were fired at us at 4 a.m. It woke everybody up: every single person in Ukraine, children and adults. We have not slept since. We took up arms, and we became a great army.

On the second day, we fought off attacks in the air, on land and at sea. Our heroic border guards on Zmiinyi Island in the Black Sea showed everyone how the war will end. When a Russian ship demanded that our guys lay down their weapons, they answered him with – well, an answer so firm, that one cannot repeat it in Parliament.* In that moment, we felt strong. It was the strength of a people who will resist the invader to the end.

On the third day, Russian troops unashamedly fired at civilians and apartment buildings. They used artillery and dropped bombs. It finally showed the world who is who: which side are a great nation, and which side are animals.

On the fourth day, we began to take prisoners. But we did not lose our dignity. We did not abuse them. We treated them like people. Because, on the fourth day of this shameful war, we retained our humanity.

On the fifth day, the attempts to terrorise us became obvious. There was terror against cities, terror against small towns; bombs upon bombs raining down on houses, on schools, on hospitals. This

---

* When invited by Russian troops to surrender, Ukrainian soldiers on Zmiinyi Island responded with, 'Russian warship, go fuck yourself.'

war is an act of genocide. But it is an act that has not broken us. It has mobilised us, and taught us a great truth about the world.

On the sixth day, Russian missiles hit Babyn Yar. During the Second World War, Nazis killed over 100,000 people there. Eighty years later, Russia dishonoured their memories by hitting them for a second time.

On the seventh day, we realised that the Russian forces were even destroying churches. They do not understand the holy and the great as we do.

On the eighth day, the world saw Russian tanks firing at a nuclear power plant, the largest in Europe. That was when the world began to understand that this is an act of terror against us all: a great terror, in fact.

On the ninth day, a meeting of the NATO Parliamentary Assembly ended without the result we were looking for, and without a display of courage. We felt that alliances do not work; they can't even impose a no-fly zone. That is why the security guarantees in Europe must be rebuilt from scratch.

On the tenth day, unarmed Ukrainians protested everywhere in the occupied cities. They stopped armoured vehicles with their bare hands. We became invincible.

On the eleventh day, children, cities and hospitals were hit by rockets. Children had to be evacuated from a cancer ward. That was when we realised that all Ukrainians have become heroes. Hundreds of thousands of them, children and adults, entire cities strong.

On the twelfth day, when the losses of the invading army already exceeded 10,000 killed, a Russian general joined that number. It gave us confidence. For every crime and for every shameful order, someone will be held responsible – whether before the International Criminal Court, or by Ukrainian weapons.

On the thirteenth day, a child died of dehydration in Russian-occupied Mariupol. The Russian forces do not allow food or water to reach people. They have blocked the supplies, and people have started to panic. Let everyone hear the truth: in Ukraine, there are people who don't have access to water.

In these thirteen days, fifty children have been killed. Fifty lives that could have been lived to the full, taken away from us.

We were not looking for this war. Ukraine did not seek greatness. But over these last thirteen days, Ukraine has become great.

Ukraine: a country that is saving lives despite the terror of the occupiers. A country that is defending freedom despite the blows of one of the biggest armies in the world. And a country that is defending itself, despite its sky still being open to Russian missiles, planes and helicopters.

Consider a famous phrase: 'To be or not to be'. That may have been the question thirteen days ago. But it is no longer a question. Our answer is definitely, 'To be,' and to be free.

Let me remind you of words that the United Kingdom has heard before, for they are important again. 'We shall go on to the end . . . We shall fight on the seas and oceans. We shall fight with growing confidence and growing strength in the air. We shall defend our island, whatever the cost may be.

'We shall fight on the beaches, we shall fight on the landing grounds, we shall fight in the fields and in the streets, we shall fight in the hills.'

And, I want to add, we shall fight on the spoil tips, on the banks of the Kalmius and the Dnieper.

We shall never surrender.

We are thankful for all your help, and I am thankful to you, Boris Johnson, my friend. Please, increase the pressure of the sanctions against Russia. Please, recognise this country as a terrorist state. Please, make sure the Ukrainian skies are safe.

Please, do what the greatness of your country calls upon you to do.

10

'The Leader in Peace'

Address to the US Congress
Washington DC (via video link), 16 March 2022

Russia has attacked more than just our land and our cities. It has begun a brutal offensive against our values.

It threw tanks and planes against the right to life. Against our right to liberty, and to choose our own future. And against our pursuit of happiness. Russia is waging a war against our national dreams; dreams that are just like yours.

I remember the Mount Rushmore National Memorial, carved with the faces of your greatest Presidents. It honours those who laid the foundations of America as it is today. Democracy, independence, freedom, and a society that takes care of everyone who works diligently, lives honestly and respects the law. The people of Ukraine merely want the same for ourselves.

Friends, in your history books there are pages that will allow you to understand what is happening in Ukraine. Remember the terrible morning of 7 December 1941: the attack on Pearl Harbor. Remember the feeling when your sky was black from the planes attacking you.

Remember 11 September 2001, when evil tried to turn your cities into a battlefield. Remember when innocent people were attacked from the air, in a way nobody had expected and nobody could stop.

Our state now experiences this every day. Every night for three weeks – in Odesa and Kharkiv, Chernihiv and Sumy, Zhytomyr and Lviv, Mariupol and Dnipro – Russia has transformed the Ukrainian sky into a place of death, claiming the lives of thousands. Russian troops have already fired nearly a thousand missiles at Ukraine, and countless bombs. It is a terror not seen in Europe for eighty years.

I am here to ask for the world to respond to this terror. Is this too much to ask?

We ask first for a no-fly zone. Under these conditions, Russia would no longer be able to terrorise our peaceful cities, day and night. If that is too much, we suggest an alternative: weapons. You know what defence systems we need, and you know how much depends on our ability to use aircraft. The same aircraft that protect your people – your freedom – can help Ukraine, and can help Europe.

'I have a dream'. Every American knows these words. Well, today I say, 'I have a need.' Because now, these words mean the same to us as when you say, 'I have a dream.'

Know that Ukraine is grateful to the United States for its overwhelming support. For all that your state and your people have already done for our freedom. For weapons and ammunition, for training and funding, and for the economic pressure you have put on our aggressor. I am grateful to President Biden for his sincere commitment to the defence of Ukraine and to democracy around the world. And I am grateful to you for this resolution, which recognises all those who commit crimes against the Ukrainian people as war criminals. But now, in the darkest time for our country, I urge you to do more . . .

For today, it is not enough to be the leader of the nation.* Today, it is necessary to be the leader of the world. And to be the leader of the world means to be the leader in peace.

Peace in your country no longer depends only on

* From here onwards, Zelensky speaks in English.

what happens to you and your people. It depends on the strength of your allies.

It depends on your bravery, and your being ready to fight for the lives of citizens around the world. To fight for human rights and for freedom; for the right to live decently and to die only when your time comes.

It depends on not giving all these up when they are threatened by your neighbour.

Today, the Ukrainian people are not only defending Ukraine. We are also fighting for the values of Europe and the world, sacrificing our lives in the name of a better future.

That's why today the American people are helping not just Ukraine, but Europe and the planet, to keep justice in our world.

Today, I am almost forty-five years old. And in the weeks leading up to today, the hearts of more than one hundred children have stopped beating. I see no sense in my life if it cannot prevent death.

And so, as the President of my country, I am addressing President Biden. You are the leader of a great nation. I wish you to be the leader of the world.

Being the leader of the world means being the leader in peace.

22

'Tear Down This Wall!'

Address to the German Bundestag
Berlin (via video link), 17 March 2022

Over the last three weeks of war, the people of Ukraine have become convinced of something we had before only suspected. It is something you have probably not noticed yet.

It is as though you are behind the wall again. Not the Berlin Wall, but another wall in the middle of Europe: a wall between freedom and slavery. And this wall grows stronger with each bomb that falls on our land, and with every decision that is not made in the name of peace.

How did this happen? When we told you that Nord Stream* was a weapon being built in preparation for

---

* Gas pipelines connecting Russia to Germany under the Baltic Sea.

a great war, we heard in response that it was about nothing more than 'the economy'.

But it was cement for a new wall.

When we asked you what Ukraine needed to do to become a member of NATO and to secure our safety, we were told, 'That is not on the table, and will not be in the near future.' In the same way, you are delaying Ukraine's accession to the European Union. Some people think this is politics.

The truth is that it is stones: stones for a new wall.

When we were seeking preventive sanctions against Russia, we appealed to many countries in Europe; we turned to you. But we encountered resistance. We understood that you wanted to support 'the economy'.

And now, the trade routes between you and the country that has once again brought a brutal war to Europe are barbed wire over the wall: the new wall that divides Europe.

Many of you do not see what is behind this wall between the people of Europe. As a result, not everyone is fully aware of what we are going through today in Ukraine.

So I am addressing you now on behalf of Ukrainians, and on behalf of Mariupol residents – a city that Russian troops have blocked and razed to the ground.

They have destroyed everything and everyone who is there. Hundreds of thousands of people are being shelled around the clock. There is no food or water, electricity or communication, for twenty-four hours a day. It has been this way for weeks.

Russian troops do not distinguish between civilians and the military. They don't care where ordinary infrastructure is. Everything is considered a target. Yesterday, a theatre that was serving as a shelter for hundreds of people was blown up. So were a maternity hospital, a children's hospital, and many residential areas without any military facilities. The Russians do not let any humanitarian cargo into the city. For five days, Russian troops have not stopped the shelling, to deliberately prevent people from being rescued.

You can see it all. If you simply climb over this wall.

I ask you to think of what the Berlin Airlift* meant to Germans. It was possible because the sky was safe. Today, in our country, we cannot even conduct an airlift; the sky offers up only Russian missiles and air bombs.

---

* In 1948–9 the Western Allies, faced with the Soviet blockade of West Berlin, airlifted the city supplies to prevent it from falling into the Soviet sphere of influence.

A Message from Ukraine

Today, I appeal to you on behalf of older Ukrainians, many of whom escaped during the occupation of Ukraine eighty years ago and survived the war. Those who lived through Babyn Yar. It was Babyn Yar that your President, Frank-Walter Steinmeier, visited last year, on the eightieth anniversary of the tragedy. Since then, the site has been hit by Russian missiles.

The air strike killed a family visiting the Holocaust memorial on the site. They were murdered on the same ground as their forebears, eighty years later.

I appeal to you on behalf of all those who have heard politicians say, 'Never again' – and on behalf of everyone who has now seen that these words are worthless. Because once again in Europe, an invader is trying to destroy a whole people, and to destroy everything we live by and for.

I appeal to you on behalf of our military. Those who defend our state, and so defend the values that are talked about everywhere in Europe, including here in Germany. The values of freedom and equality. The right to live in liberty, and not to submit to another state that considers a foreign land its 'living space'. Why are so many other states more supportive of us than you are?

For this is the wall I speak of. The wall that some

77

of you don't notice, even though we are hammering against it while fighting to save our people.

I am grateful to all Germans who offer us support. To the ordinary German people who are sincerely helping Ukrainians. To the journalists who do their job honestly, showing the evil that Russia has brought to us. And to the German businesspeople who put morality and humanity above accounting and above 'the economy'.

And I am grateful to the politicians who are still trying to break this wall. Those who choose life without Russian money over the deaths of Ukrainian children. Who support strengthening the sanctions that can bring peace to Ukraine, and peace to Europe. And who know that an embargo on trade with Russia is needed . . . In other words, I am grateful to those who are taller than any wall – and who understand that when it comes to saving people, it is the strongest who bear the greatest responsibility.

But know that it is difficult for us to keep going without your help and the help of the world. It is difficult to defend Ukraine – to defend Europe – without the support you can offer. After the destruction of Kharkiv, for the second time in eighty years. After the bombing of Chernihiv, Sumy and Donbas, for the second time in eighty years. After thousands of people have been tortured and killed, for the second time in eighty years.

Otherwise, what is the meaning of the historic responsibility that still goes unredeemed eighty years later? How will you stop a new debt from being incurred from behind this new wall – a debt that would again demand redemption?

Ronald Reagan once said in Berlin, 'Tear down this wall!' I want to tell you the same. Chancellor Scholz, tear down this wall!

Give Germans the leadership they deserve, and which your descendants will be proud of.

Support us. Support peace. Support every Ukrainian.

Help us stop the war.

12

'Indifference Kills'

Address to the Israeli Knesset
Jerusalem (via video link), 20 March 2022

I want to begin by reminding you of the words of a great woman from Kyiv, Golda Meir.* 'We intend to remain alive. Our neighbours want to see us dead. This is not a question that leaves much room for compromise.'

These words are famous. Every Jew has heard them. Many other Ukrainians have too, and certainly no fewer Russians.

So I don't need to convince you how intertwined the stories of Ukrainians and Jews have always been – in the past and now, in this terrible time. We are in different countries and in completely different

---

* Israeli politician (1898–1978), Prime Minister of Israel from 1969 to 1974.

conditions. But the threat is the same. In both cases, the total destruction of a people, state, culture. They even want to deprive us of our names: Ukraine, Israel.

I want you to feel what we feel. Think of 24 February, the first day of Russia's invasion of Ukraine. It is a day that has twice gone down in history, both times as a tragedy. A tragedy for Ukrainians, for Jews; for Europe, for the world.

On 24 February 1920, the National Socialist Workers' Party of Germany was founded. It would go on to take millions of lives, destroy entire countries — even attempt to kill entire peoples.

On 24 February 2022, exactly 102 years later, a criminal order was issued to launch a full-scale Russian invasion of Ukraine. This invasion has claimed thousands of lives, and left millions homeless. Many are exiles in neighbouring countries: Poland, Slovakia, Romania, Germany, the Czech Republic, the Baltic States and dozens of other nations.

Now, our people are scattered around the world. They are searching for security. They are searching for peace. Just as you once searched.

This Russian invasion of Ukraine is not just a military operation, as Moscow claims. It is a large and treacherous war, aimed at destroying a people.

The goal is to eliminate our children and our families, our state and our cities, our communities and our culture: everything that makes us Ukrainians. Russian troops are doing this deliberately, in front of the whole world.

That is why I have the right to draw this parallel. Our history and your history. Our war for survival and the Second World War.

Just listen to what the Kremlin says. They use terms you have encountered before. When the Nazis raided Europe, they didn't only want to conquer nations. They wanted to destroy everything and everyone, to leave nothing of you and of us behind: neither the name nor the trace. They called it the 'final solution' to the Jewish 'issue'. You remember that, and I know you will never forget.

But listen to the noises coming from Moscow now. Hear the return of those words: 'final solution'. But this time in reference to us, the 'Ukrainian issue'.

This was said openly, at a meeting in Moscow. It is available on official websites. It was quoted in the Russian state media. They say that without war against us, they would not be able to ensure a 'final solution' to the supposed problems of their own security.

The very same words as were used eighty years ago.

People of Israel, you have seen Russian missiles hit Babyn Yar. You know what kind of land it is: more than 100,000 Holocaust victims are buried there. In Kyiv there is an ancient Jewish cemetery. Russian missiles have hit that too. On the first day of this war, Russian projectiles hit our city of Uman. It is a city visited by tens of thousands of Israelis every year, for a pilgrimage to the tomb of Nachman of Breslov. What will be left of such places after this terrible war?

I am sure that every word of my address causes a pang of pain in your hearts. Because you feel what I am talking about. Can you explain, then, why we still must turn to the world for help? We are still asking you for assistance, even simply to grant entry visas.

What is it? Indifference? Calculation? Or a desire to mediate, to avoid picking sides? I will leave you to answer these questions. But I will note only one thing: indifference kills. Calculation can be dangerous. And mediation can only be between states, not between good and evil.

Everyone in Israel knows that your missile defence system is the best. Everyone on earth knows that your weapons are strong. You know how to defend the interests of your people.

And so you can help us protect our lives, too. The lives of Ukrainians; the lives of Ukrainian Jews.

I could keep asking why we can't get weapons from you. Or why Israel has not imposed strong sanctions against Russia, nor put pressure on Russian business. But it is up to you, dear brothers and sisters, to choose the answer. And the people of Israel will have to live with this answer.

Ukrainians made their choice. Eighty years ago, Ukrainians rescued Jews. That is why the Righteous Among the Nations still live in our country.

People of Israel, you now have such a choice.

PART IV
OUR NATION

'What will bring the end of the war? We used to say "peace". Now we say "victory".'

UKRAINE'S RESISTANCE TOOK the world by surprise. The government did not collapse. The President did not flee. And, in many parts of the country, the Ukrainian military pushed the Russian forces back. But these victories were always bitter-sweet. With every new city liberated, evidence of Russian war crimes mounted. This was not just a struggle of armies; it was a struggle of values. In Zelensky's speeches from April 2022 onwards, he would emphasise how these values had brought Ukrainians together as a nation. Putin had tried to destroy a people, and he had failed. From the ruins of the war, Ukraine had emerged more defiant and united than ever before: 'Not a nation born, but a nation reborn.'

23

'How Did This Become Possible?'

Address to the Ukrainian people
Kyiv, 3 April 2022

My address today begins without a greeting. I do not want to utter any more words than are necessary.

Presidents do not usually record addresses of this kind. But today I have no choice, after what was revealed in Bucha and the other cities from which the occupiers were expelled. Hundreds of people killed. Civilians tortured and executed. Corpses on the streets. Landmines across the city, even inside the bodies of the dead. The effects of looting visible everywhere.

Concentrated evil has come to our land. We have been invaded by murderers, torturers, rapists and looters. People who call themselves the army, and who deserve only death for what they have done.

I want the mother of every Russian soldier to see

the bodies of those killed in Bucha, in Irpin, in Hostomel. What did they do wrong? Why were they killed?

What did the man who was riding his bicycle down the street do? Or the ordinary civilians in a peaceful city who were tortured to death? Why were women strangled after their earrings were ripped out? Why were women raped and killed in front of children? Why were their corpses desecrated? Why were people's bodies crushed with tanks?

What did Bucha do to Russia? How did this become possible?

Russian mothers: even if you raised looters, how did they also become butchers? You can't have been unaware of what lay in your children's minds. You couldn't have missed their lack of humanity. That they were becoming people without soul and without heart. People who killed deliberately and with pleasure.

I want the leaders of the russian federation to see how their orders are being carried out. They share the responsibility. They are culpable for the arms torn off by explosives, and for the people shot in the back of the head with their hands tied.

This is how the Russian state will now be seen. This is your image. Your culture and humanity died along with the Ukrainian men and women you killed.

I have approved the creation of a special judicial mechanism in Ukraine. It will investigate every crime committed by the occupiers of Ukrainian territory, drawing upon the joint efforts of national and international experts, investigators, prosecutors and judges. And it will hold those who participated in this terrible war against the Ukrainian people accountable. The Ministry of Foreign Affairs, the Office of the Prosecutor General, the National Police, the Security Service, the Intelligence Service and other state bodies will make every effort to ensure that it is operational immediately. I call on all our citizens and friends of Ukraine around the world to join in these efforts, and so help us achieve justice.

The world has seen war crimes before, committed on many occasions and on many continents. But we must make the war crimes of the Russian military the last time this evil plagues the earth. Everyone guilty of such crimes will be included in a special Book of Torturers.* They will be found and they will be punished.

Ukrainians, we have driven the enemy from many parts of our country. But Russian troops still occupy

---

* Database launched to collect information about war crimes committed during the Russian invasion.

others. And after the occupiers have been expelled, even worse things may be found there: more deaths, more torture victims. This is the nature of the Russian military. They are bastards, they cannot do otherwise. They have their orders to follow.

Ukraine's allies will be informed in detail about what has happened in the temporarily occupied territories. The war crimes in Bucha and other cities during the Russian occupation will be considered by the UN Security Council on Tuesday. There will certainly be a new package of sanctions against Russia.

But that is not enough. We need to draw wider conclusions: not only about Russia, but also about the political context that allowed this evil to come to our land.

Today is the fourteenth anniversary of the NATO summit in Bucharest. The summit offered an opportunity to take Ukraine out of the 'grey zone' in Eastern Europe. The 'grey zone' between NATO and Russia. The 'grey zone' in which Moscow thinks they are allowed to do anything, even to commit the most horrific war crimes.

In 2008, during talks about whether Ukraine might become a member of NATO, the Alliance's intention to refuse our country was concealed. They thought that by refusing Ukraine, they would be able to appease Russia; to convince Russia to respect Ukraine and live peacefully beside us.

In the fourteen years since that miscalculation, Ukraine has experienced a revolution and eight years of war in Donbas. Now, we are fighting for our lives in the most horrific conflict in Europe since the Second World War. I invite Mrs Merkel and Mr Sarkozy to visit Bucha. Let them come and see what their concessions to Russia have led to fourteen years later. Come and see the tortured Ukrainians with their own eyes.

Do not misunderstand me. We do not blame the West. We do not blame anyone but the Russian military personnel who did this, and the people who gave them their orders. But we have the right to talk about indecision, and to identify the path that led us to Bucha, to Hostomel, to Kharkiv, to Mariupol.

For we are decisive. No matter whether we are in a security alliance or stand alone, we understand one thing: we must be strong.

Fourteen years ago, in Bucharest, Russia's leader told the West that there was no such state as Ukraine. But we have proved that there is. There long has been such a country and there long will be.

Know that we will not hide behind the strength of the world's most powerful nations. We will not go cap in hand to anyone. We should not have had to ask for help with weapons to protect ourselves from the evil that came to our land. All the necessary weapons should have been given to us without us having to ask. The world should have realised what evil had come, and what horror it had brought with it.

We see what is at stake in this war. We know what it is we are defending.

On the one hand, there are the standards of the Ukrainian army, moral and professional. It is an army of the highest principles: one that many other armies should learn from. These are the standards of the Ukrainian people.

On the other, there are the standards of the Russian occupiers. It is the difference between good and evil. It is the difference between Europe and a black hole, one that wants to absorb everything into its darkness.

We will win this war. Even if individual politicians are unable to overcome their indecision, whether now or in the future. Already, we are working to bring Bucha back to life: to restore the electricity supply and the water supply, to restart the work of medical institutions, to rebuild the infrastructure, to return to people their security.

Russia has been expelled, and Ukraine is coming back. And bringing life back with it.

Earlier today, I visited some of our wounded warriors in the hospital of the Border Guard Service of Ukraine. I presented state awards to all eight of them. I also presented an award to a medical service officer, a leading military traumatologist in Ukraine who has already saved the lives of many of our defenders. In total, forty-one border guards received state awards.

It was the servicemen of the State Border Guard Service who first fought back when the offensive began on 24 February. Now, our troops are returning to the state border as we expel the occupiers.

I know the time will come when the whole state border of Ukraine will be restored. And for this to happen sooner, we must all remain focused. We must be ready to face evil. And we must be prepared to respond to every criminal act against Ukraine, our people, and our freedom.

Evil will be punished.

14

'God Save Ukraine'

Easter Address

Kyiv, 24 April 2022

Today is a great holiday, and I am in a great place: St Sophia's Cathedral. This cathedral, first built a thousand years ago, stands on the site where the army of Kyivan Rus' defeated the Pechenegs. It was not destroyed by the invasion of the Mongol Horde, nor by the Nazi occupation. It withstood everything.

Today, we have faith in a new victory for Ukraine. We have faith that, once again, we will not be destroyed by any invading evil.

We are enduring dark times. Although today is a day of light, most of us are not wearing colourful clothes. But we are fighting for light. We are fighting for the truth. And in that, God and the light of heaven are on our side.

Above me is Oranta, depicting the patron saint of

humanity.* And just as she is above me, she is above us all. She stands here, in the unbreakable wall of the main stronghold of our nation, Kyiv . . . Above the image of Oranta are words from the Psalms. 'God dwells in that city; it cannot be destroyed. From the very break of day, God will protect it.' Today, we all believe that our dawn is coming soon.

'Oranta' means 'one who prays'. And for the last two months we have all been praying. The Resurrection of Christ symbolises the victory of life over death. And today, each of us prays for the same thing. We ask God to save Ukraine.

Protect those who protect us: our military, our national guard, our border guards, our territorial defence, our intelligence services. Save them, our warriors of light.

Help those who help them: our volunteers and anyone who cares for Ukraine, from here and around the world . . .

Save the lives of those who save the lives of others: our medics, our firefighters, our rescuers, our sappers. Let life be not only a symbol of Easter. Let life win the battle against death every day of the year.

Look after our mothers. Give endurance to those

* Mosaic of the Virgin Mary inside St Sophia's Cathedral.

who are waiting for a son or daughter to return from the war. Give fortitude to those who have lost children on the front line. Give strength to those who have lost children in the peaceful cities and villages to which Russia has brought death.

Grant health to our grandmothers for many more years. Grant them the chance to see their loved ones again. To see peace and victory. To see justice. And to see the happy old age that the invaders are trying to steal from them. For today, instead of knitting scarves and jumpers for their grandchildren, they weave camouflage nets.

Protect our fathers and our grandfathers. The men who once told their grandchildren about the last war, and now send them to the new one. The men who built this country, and today are seeing it destroyed. Let them see our land liberated and rebuilt, and give us the strength to rebuild it.

Take care of our children. Give every boy and every girl a happy childhood, adulthood and old age – a life long enough to rid themselves of their terrible youthful memories of war. The terrifying games they have been forced to play have no place in a child's life. Hide-and-seek, except they hide from bombs. Running not around a playground, but to shelter from gunshots. Travelling across the country, not to a holiday site but from their destroyed homes.

Save all Ukrainians. We did not attack anyone, so defend us. We have never destroyed another nation, so do not let anyone destroy us. We have never seized another people's land, so do not let anyone seize ours.

And save Ukraine. Save us on the right and left banks of the Dnipro. For when winter ended, spring did not come. The frost of winter came to our homes, and at dawn we were brought nothing but darkness.

God, we know that you will not forget the actions of those who have ignored your commandments. We know you will not forget about the atrocities in Bucha, Irpin, Borodyanka, Hostomel. And we also know that you will not forget those who survived these brutal crimes. Bring joy to them and all the people of Ukraine.

We know you will not forget about the noise of the bombs that fell on Chernihiv, Mykolaiv, Kherson, Sumy, Kharkiv, Izyum, Kramatorsk and Volnovakha, Popasna. Let these cities instead hear the sound of Ukraine's victory.

We know you will not forget about Mariupol and its heroic defenders. The invaders might destroy the city's walls, but they cannot destroy its foundations:

the morale of our warriors; the morale of the whole country.

Today, we see terrible images of war. But let us soon see a happy picture of peace.

Today, we are going through the hardest of trials. But let it soon reach the just verdict: the return of life, happiness and prosperity to Ukraine.

Today, our hearts are full of fierce fury and our souls overflow with hatred for the invaders. But do not let this fury destroy us from within. Turn it into victories without. Transform our rage into a force with which to defeat evil.

Save us from strife and from division. Do not let us lose our unity.

Strengthen our will and our spirit. Do not let us lose ourselves.

Do not let us lose our longing for freedom. And do not let us lose our passion for this righteous struggle. Do not let us lose our hope of victory, our self-esteem, our freedom.

Do not let us lose our Ukraine. Do not let us lose our faith.

Ukrainians, last year we celebrated Easter at home because of the pandemic. This year, once again, we are unable to celebrate the Resurrection as we used to. We are afflicted now by another virus: the plague of war.

But know that last year's illness and this one's are united by one truth: that nothing can defeat Ukraine. And so this great holiday gives us hope.

It offers us faith that light will overcome darkness, good will overcome evil, life will overcome death.

And it offers us faith that Ukraine will win.

15

'Never Again?'

Address on the Ukrainian Day of
Remembrance and Reconciliation
Borodyanka, 8 May 2022

Can spring arrive in black and white?

Can the cold of February go on for ever?

Can words of peace lose their meaning?

Ukraine knows that the answers to all these questions can be 'yes'.

Every year on 8 May, together with the entire civilised world, we honour all who defended the planet from Nazism during the Second World War. We remember the millions of lives lost, destinies crippled, souls tortured.

We remember the millions of reasons to say to evil, 'Never again.'

We have long understood the price our ancestors paid so that we can say these words. We have long known how important it is to preserve them and pass them on to posterity. But until now, we had no idea that our generation would witness their desecration.

They are not, it turns out, words of truth for everyone.

This year, we say 'Never again' differently. We hear 'Never again' differently. It sounds painful, cruel – now without an exclamation mark, but with a question mark. You say 'Never again'? Tell that to the people of Ukraine.

On 24 February, the word 'never' was erased. It was shot and bombed by hundreds of missiles at 4 a.m., which woke up the whole of Ukraine. Then, all we heard was 'again'.

The city of Borodyanka is one of the many victims of this crime. I give this address standing before the proof. It is not a military facility nor a secret base, but a simple nine-storey block of flats. Can it pose a security threat to Russia? To a nation that takes up one eighth of the planet's land, to the world's second-largest army, to a nuclear state? Could any question be more absurd?

Consider the 250-kilogram bombs with which a superpower shelled this small town. In that moment, the town was rendered mute. Today, it cannot say,

'Never again.' Today, it cannot say anything. Yet here, everything is clear without words.

Just look at this house. There used to be walls here. They once had photos on them with images of those who went through the hell of war. The fifty men from this town who were sent to Germany for forced labour. The people who were burned alive when the Nazis set 100 houses here on fire. The 250 Borodyanka soldiers who died on the fronts of the Second World War, out of the nearly 1,000 residents of this town who fought and defeated Nazism.

They fought to say, 'Never again.'

They fought for their children's future.

They fought for the life that was here until 24 February.

Imagine the people in these apartments going to bed. Imagine them wishing each other good night, turning off the light and hugging their loved ones.

They closed their eyes and they fell asleep. They did not know that not everyone would see tomorrow.

They slept soundly and dreamt. They did not know that in a few hours they would be awoken by missile explosions, and that some would not wake at all.

'Never again'? Now, the word 'never' has been dropped. It was taken during the so-called 'special operation'. Russia looked us in the eyes and stabbed a knife into the heart of 'Never again' . . . Until the monsters of our past began to reappear.

Ukraine has not forgotten the occupation of our cities eighty years ago. Many are now experiencing a second occupation; some, such as Mariupol, a third. During two years of occupation, the Nazis killed 10,000 civilians there. In two months of occupation, Russia has killed 20,000.

Decades after the Second World War, darkness has returned to Ukraine.

Our cities are drained of colour, turning black and white again.

Evil has returned. In a different uniform, under different slogans, but for the same purpose.

A bloody reconstruction of Nazism has taken place in Ukraine. A reconstruction of the old ideas, actions, words and symbols. A reconstruction of its atrocities and its attempts to imbue evil with some legitimate purpose. Sometimes, this reconstruction even attempts to surpass its 'teacher' to become the greatest evil in human history. It aims to set a new record for xenophobia, hatred and racism, and for the number of victims it can harm.

'Never again'? That was the anthem of a civilised world. But someone sang it out of tune. They distorted the melody of 'Never again' with notes of doubt. And eventually, the song of 'Never again' went silent.

So now, all countries that experienced Nazism first-hand are experiencing a terrible déjà vu. Nations that have been branded 'inferior', or as slaves without the right to their own state, or as people who should not exist at all. They see the horrors of their past resurface.

They hear statements that exalt one nation and erase others; which claim that your people do not really exist, and therefore you have no rights. They hear the language of evil again.

And together, these countries realise a painful truth. That we have not lasted even a century with our 'Never again'. We lasted a mere seventy-seven years. We did not notice the evil as it was reborn.

This truth is understood by all countries who support Ukraine today. Despite the new mask which the beast is wearing, they recognise him. Unlike some, they remember what our ancestors fought for and against. Unlike some, they did not get confused about right and wrong. They remember.

The Poles have not forgotten on whose land the Nazis began their march, and fired the opening shot of the Second World War. They have not forgotten how evil first accuses you, provokes you, calls you an aggressor, and then attacks at 4 a.m. while calling it self-defence. They see their experiences repeated on our land. When they recall the Nazi-destroyed Warsaw, and they see what was done to Mariupol, they remember.

The British have not forgotten how the Nazis wiped out Coventry, which was bombed forty-one times. They have not forgotten the Luftwaffe's so-called 'Moonlight Sonata', in which the city was under constant air-raid for eleven hours. They have not forgotten how Coventry's historic centre, how its factories, how St Michael's Cathedral were destroyed. When they see the missiles hit Kharkiv and damage its historic centre, its factories and the Assumption Cathedral, they remember.

They have not forgotten London being bombed for fifty-seven nights in a row. When they recall how V-2 bombs hit Belfast, Portsmouth and Liverpool, and they see cruise missiles hit Mykolaiv, Kramatorsk and Chernihiv; when they recall how Birmingham was bombed, and they see its sister city Zaporizhzhia under attack, they remember.

The French have not forgotten Oradour-sur-Glane, where the SS burned 500 women and children alive. They have not forgotten the mass hangings in Tulle, the massacre in the village of Ascq, the thousands protesting at a resistance rally in occupied Lille. They see what has been done in Bucha, Irpin, Borodyanka, Volnovakha and Trostyanets. They see the occupation of Kherson, Melitopol, Berdyansk and other cities where people do not give up. They see how thousands of Ukrainians go to peaceful rallies where all the occupiers can do is shoot at civilians. They remember.

The Dutch have not forgotten how Rotterdam became the first city to be completely destroyed under 97 tons of Nazi bombs. The Czechs have not forgotten how, in less than a day, the Nazis destroyed Lidice, leaving only ashes where the village once stood. They saw how Popasna was destroyed, with nothing but ashes left. The Greeks have not forgotten how they survived massacres and executions, the blockade and the Great Famine. They remember.

The Americans have not forgotten how they fought evil on two fronts. They recall the struggles of Pearl Harbor and of Dunkirk alongside their allies. Together, we are going through new battles, but no less difficult ones. They remember.

Holocaust survivors have not forgotten. They recall how one nation can hate another. They remember. Lithuanians, Latvians, Estonians, Danes, Georgians, Armenians, Belgians, Norwegians and countless others have not forgotten. All those who suffered from Nazism on their land and all those who defeated it as part of the anti-Hitler coalition. They remember.

And yet there are those who – having survived all these crimes, having lost millions of people, having fought and won – have desecrated their victory.

The man who has orchestrated the shelling of Ukraine. The man who has dropped bombs upon cities that were liberated by his very ancestors, along with our own. The man who has spat in the face of his own Victory Day celebration by putting the torturers of Bucha at its centre. The man who has demeaned all mankind.

But he has forgotten the most important point. Evil always loses.

Fellow Ukrainians, today we pay homage to all those who defended their homeland and the world from Nazism. We remember the feat of the Ukrainian people and their contribution to the victory against Hitler. They experienced explosions, shots, trenches, wounds; famine, bombing, blockades, mass executions, punitive operations, occupation; concentration camps, gas chambers, yellow stars, ghettos, Babyn Yar, Khatyn, captivity, forced labour.

They died so that each of us could know what these

words mean from history books, not from our own lives.

But their experiences are being repeated. And this dishonours them all.

Yet know this: the truth will win. And we will get through everything . . .

We will get through this winter, which began on 24 February and continues now on 8 May, but will definitely end – for the Ukrainian sun will melt it again.

We will meet the dawn together with the whole country. One day soon, loved ones will be together again.

Our flag will fly over the occupied cities again.

Our nation will be reunited and there will be peace again.

And the world will no longer dream in black and white. It will only dream in blue and yellow.

This is what our ancestors fought for.

16

'A Free People'

Address on Ukrainian Independence Day
Kyiv, 24 August 2022

The free people of an independent Ukraine.

These seven words say everything. Seven little words – but how much meaning they hold today, on day 182 of the full-scale war. How many symbols and ideas, triumphs and losses, joys and pains are contained in these words. And how much truth is in them, too.

They capture a truth it is impossible to dispute. That we are the free people of an independent Ukraine. A truth about the present: that after six months of attempts to destroy us, we are still the free people of an independent Ukraine. And it is also the truth about our future: that we will remain the free people of an independent Ukraine.

Six months ago, Russia declared war on us. On

24 February the whole of Ukraine heard explosions and gunshots. Ukraine was not supposed to hear the words 'Happy Independence Day' on 24 August. On 24 February, we were told, 'You have no chance.' On 24 August, we can say, 'Happy Independence Day, Ukraine.'

Over these six months, we have changed history, we have changed the world, and above all, we have changed ourselves. Today, we know for certain who is really our comrade and our friend, and who is not even a casual acquaintance. We know who maintained their name and reputation, and who was on the side of the terrorists. Who doesn't really want us, and who keeps the door open to us. At last we have learned who is who.

And the whole world has learned who Ukrainians are, too. What *Ukraine* is. Never again will anyone say, 'It is somewhere over there, near Russia.'

We started to respect ourselves. We came to understand that while others might offer help and support, only we would fight for our independence. And so we united.

We didn't have HIMARS yet,* but we had people

* US-built missile system in use by the Ukrainian military from June 2022 onwards.

willing to stop tanks with their bare hands. Our allies were not prepared to impose a no-fly zone, but we had people willing to protect their native land with their own lives.

The courage of the Ukrainian people has inspired the whole world. It has renewed humanity's hope that justice has not completely disappeared from our world.

And they have shown that it is not force that wins, but truth. Not money, but values. Not oil, but people.

Yesterday the world was divided. In the global response to the Covid-19 pandemic it was every man for himself. Ukraine changed that in just six months. From now on, every history textbook will have a new section: 'When Ukraine united the world'. When democracy grew teeth again. When tyranny received an answer in the language it understands.

People said that Europe was no longer a player in international politics. That Europe was weak, divided, passive, sleepy. But Ukraine has invigorated the entire continent. Today, the people of Europe have taken to the squares. Today, Europe has introduced tough sanctions. Today, Europe unanimously recognises that Ukraine is a future member of the EU.

Big business has realised that money still smells: it can carry the stench of blood, cinders, death.

Today, corporations are leaving the Russian market en masse. People have become more important than lost profits.

Never before has public opinion had such an influence on politicians. Today, it is people who determine the behaviour of their governments. Nations are ashamed to be indifferent, inactive or slow. They are ashamed to make vague commitments or speak in overly diplomatic language. They are ashamed not to support Ukraine.

And they are ashamed to say they are tired of Ukraine. Tiredness, perhaps, would be more comfortable: it would allow the world to close its eyes. But today that is not what we hear from world leaders and from citizens. We hear, 'We will be with you until the end, until your victory.'

Ukrainians, this day has always been our main holiday. It has long been a chance to pay tribute to those who have fought for Ukraine's independence, and to salute the blue-and-yellow flag. It has long been the moment when we put our hands to our hearts while singing the national anthem, and proudly say, 'Glory to Ukraine!' and 'Glory to Heroes!'

On 24 February, we had to prove the truth of these words with deeds. On that day, the second all-Ukrainian referendum took place.* Again, the question was independence. Again, the verdict was decisive. But this time it was necessary to say 'yes' to independence not on the ballot, but in the soul and in the conscience. This time, we went not to the polling booth, but to the military commissariats, the territorial defence units, the volunteer movements, the information corps – or some simply worked where they were already, steadily and conscientiously, for our common goal.

We all changed. Some people were born again: as a person, as a citizen or simply as a Ukrainian. And some 'Ukrainians' disappeared into thin air. They did not die, they simply dissolved: as a person, as a citizen, as a Ukrainian. Perhaps that is no bad thing. We will not hinder one another any more. For we all made a choice. Some chose Mariupol, others Monaco.† But we know who the majority are. We stand together, at last.

A new nation that emerged on 24 February at 4 a.m. Not a nation born, but a nation reborn.

---

* An independence referendum was held in Ukraine on 1 December 1991.
† Some of the most affluent Ukrainians moved to Monaco in the months around the outbreak of war.

A nation that didn't cry, didn't scream, didn't get scared. A nation that didn't run away, didn't give up, didn't forget.

A nation whose flag will soon fly everywhere it belongs. It will fly in Donbas and in Crimea. The enemy thought we would greet them with flowers and champagne. Instead, they were greeted with Molotov cocktails. They expected the claps and cheers of Ukrainians, but instead heard only the thunderclaps of weapons.

The occupiers believed that within a few days their army would be on parade in central Kyiv. Today, you can see their 'parade' on Khreshchatyk. There is only one form in which enemy equipment appears in the centre of Kyiv: burned, wrecked and destroyed.

It doesn't matter to us what kind of army you have, what matters to us is our land. We will fight for it until the end.

We have held on for six months. It has been difficult, but we have clenched our fists and fought for our lives. Every new day brings a new reason not to give up. Having gone through so much, we have no right not to reach the end.

What will bring the end of the war? We used to say 'peace'. Now we say 'victory'.

We will not reach an understanding with the terrorists. They came to 'defend' the Russian language, yet killed thousands of people they came to 'liberate'. Johnson,* who speaks English, makes much more sense to us – is much closer to us – than the murderers, rapists and looters who have committed these crimes in Russian.

And when we do sit around the negotiating table, it will not be because of fear, with a gun pointed at our head. Because for us, the most terrible steel is not within missiles, aircraft and tanks – but in shackles. We would rather live in trenches than live in chains.

And we will put our hands up only once, when we raise them to celebrate our victory. As the whole of Ukraine. We do not bargain away our lands and our people. Ukraine means *all* of Ukraine. All twenty-five regions, without any 'concessions' or 'compromises'. We no longer recognise such words; they were destroyed by missiles on 24 February.

Donbas is Ukraine. And it will return to us, whatever the path may be. Crimea is Ukraine. And it will return to us, whatever the path may be.

* Boris Johnson, Prime Minister of the UK until September 2022, was on a visit to Kyiv at the time this address was given.

Russians, you don't want your soldiers to die? Free our lands. You don't want your mothers to cry? Free our lands. These are our terms, clear and simple.

The free people of an independent Ukraine. We are spending this day in many different places. Some are in trenches and dugouts, in tanks and IFVs, at sea and in the air, fighting for independence on the front line. Others are on our roads, in cars, trucks and trains, fighting for independence by delivering what is necessary to those at the front. And still others are on their mobiles and laptops, fighting for independence by raising funds – so that those on the road have something to bring to those who are fighting.

We are facing this day in different circumstances, conditions and even in different time zones, but with one goal: the preservation of our independence and the victory of Ukraine.

We are united. Happy Independence Day. Glory to Ukraine.

About United24

All President Zelensky's proceeds from *A Message from Ukraine* – amounting to at least 60p per copy of the print edition sold in the UK – will go to United24, his initiative to collect donations in support of Ukraine.

Funds received by United24 will be transferred to the official accounts of the National Bank of Ukraine, and allocated by government ministries to cover their most pressing needs.

United24 is run by the government of Ukraine. For more information, visit u24.gov.ua.